To

....

From

....

Date

....

Occasion

....

One Minute

— WITH GOD —

A Year-Long Devotional Journal

DaySpring

LIVE YOUR FAITH

One Minute with God: A Year-Long Devotional Journal
Copyright © 2018 by DaySpring
First Edition, February 2018

Published by:

P.O. Box 1010
Siloam Springs, AR 72761
dayspring.com

Printed in China.

Written by Trieste Vaillancourt
Designed by Jessica Wei
Key Contributors: Linn Carlson, Marsha Van Wyngarden, Ann Woodruff

Prime: 10977
ISBN: 978-1-68408-564-4

Nothing is outside of God's jurisdiction. There's nothing He doesn't see, know, or have His hand in. Even the hard things. It's all within His reach.

The counsel of the Lord stands forever,
the plans of His heart from generation to generation.
PSALM 33:11

But what God asks, He can always deliver. When He says, "Do not be anxious," we can be confident that He's got a way for joy and thanksgiving to replace feelings of fear and worry. It's up to us to ask for and receive His grace for the moment.

Be anxious for nothing, but in everything by prayer and supplication
with thanksgiving let your requests be made known to God.
And the peace of God, which surpasses all comprehension,
will guard your hearts and your minds in Christ Jesus.
PHILIPPIANS 4:6-7

JANUARY 3

When we balance our willingness with God's strength, there's no limit to what we can do together.

He has said to me, "My grace is sufficient for you,
for power is perfected in weakness." Most gladly,
therefore, I will rather boast about my weaknesses,
so that the power of Christ may dwell in me.

II CORINTHIANS 12:9

Trusting God takes leaning in, asking tough questions, and believing extravagantly.

Who is there who speaks and it comes to pass,
unless the Lord has commanded it?
LAMENTATIONS 3:37

JANUARY 5

No matter what, you can go about today knowing that if you love the Lord, you are favored in His eyes.

The Lord favors those who fear Him,
those who wait for His lovingkindness.
PSALM 147:11

Being authentic, sharing our imperfect moments, and praying together are some of the best ways to strengthen our relationships and build trust with one another.

Therefore, confess your sins to one another,
and pray for one another so that you may be healed.
The effective prayer of a righteous man
can accomplish much.
JAMES 5:16

As we grow deeper with Jesus, we experience the life-creating love that sets us free. It's a process. It can be messy at times. But with Jesus, we are always becoming more and more like Him.

I count all things to be loss in view of
the surpassing value of knowing Christ Jesus my Lord,
for whom I have suffered the loss of all things,
and count them but rubbish so that I may gain Christ.

PHILIPPIANS 3:8

With God, we always have VIP access. All the way in. Anytime, anyplace, for any reason. No special badges or ID: if you know Jesus, you've got all the permission you need.

Therefore let us draw near with confidence
to the throne of grace, so that we may receive
mercy and find grace to help in time of need.
HEBREWS 4:16

Hope is God's specialty. He invented it. When things looked bleak, Jesus came along bearing all the possibility of freedom and eternal life.

Now may the God of hope fill you
with all joy and peace in believing,
so that you will abound in hope
by the power of the Holy Spirit.
ROMANS 15:13

Your Father watches over you with more love than you could ever imagine, and more tenderness than your heart could ever hold.

He will not allow your foot to slip;
He who keeps you will not slumber...
The Lord will guard your going out and
your coming in from this time forth and forever.

PSALM 121:3, 8

JANUARY 11

Batteries eventually give up, but we have an unending source of power and strength from God! His power has a built-in recharge. All we need to do is stay plugged in and connected to Him.

Do you not know? Have you not heard?
The Everlasting God, the Lord,
the Creator of the ends of the earth
does not become weary or tired.
His understanding is inscrutable.
ISAIAH 40:28

No matter how circumstances may seem, good or bad—our God
has the reins, because He reigns.

Who has announced this from of old?
Who has long since declared it? Is it not I, the Lord?
And there is no other God besides Me,
A righteous God and a Savior;
There is none except Me.
ISAIAH 45:21

Take heart. You're not alone. And as long as you aim to love God well, He will continue to do a good work in you.

For those whom He foreknew, He also predestined
to become conformed to the image of His Son,
so that He would be the firstborn among many brethren.
ROMANS 8:29

Worry is a life-stealer, a fun-thief. God suggests we not worry, because there's no good that comes from it. All the good comes from living expectantly for our amazing God to be His amazing self.

Who of you by being worried
can add a single hour to his life?
MATTHEW 6:27

Trust *is like stepping onto a roller coaster and raising your hands way into the air. You can be sure you're safe and buckled into God's love. Try letting go on purpose today, and see what adventures unfold.*

Commit your way to the Lord, trust also in Him,
and He will do it. He will bring forth your righteousness
as the light and your judgment as the noonday.
PSALM 37:5-6

Resting in Jesus isn't too unlike resting on a beach, in a hammock, with a cool glass of water and a good book in hand. Your mind releases its worries—to Jesus. Your body relaxes, as if wrapped in strong arms. Your thoughts turn to all the good qualities of the One who loves you more than anything.

Come to Me, all who are weary and heavy-laden,
and I will give you rest.
MATTHEW 11:28

God's idea of success isn't always the top rung of the corporate ladder, or the best voice in the talent show. He looks at us from the inside out, and loves seeing our motivations in line with His own.

Do not store up for yourselves treasures on earth,
where moth and rust destroy, and where thieves break in and steal.
But store up for yourselves treasures in heaven,
where neither moth nor rust destroys,
and where thieves do not break in or steal.
MATTHEW 6:19-20

It can be a challenge to live out the love of Jesus when circumstances are testing our emotions and patience. But every time we choose love, everyone wins.

In speech, conduct, love, faith and purity,
show yourself an example of those who believe.
I TIMOTHY 4:12

Emotions, circumstances, and—of course—people, can cause us to wonder what to do next. But like a girl and her compass, we can turn to the Word for next steps. There's never a time when kindness, love, and forgiveness are a bad path to take.

As those who have been chosen of God, holy and beloved,
put on a heart of compassion, kindness, humility,
gentleness and patience; bearing with one another,
and forgiving each other, whoever has a complaint against anyone;
just as the Lord forgave you, so also should you.
COLOSSIANS 3:12-13

Once forgiven, your past trouble disappears. No matter how bad it felt to you. No sin can remain, under the blood of Jesus.

I will forgive their iniquity,
and their sin I will remember no more.
JEREMIAH 31:34

God is often referred to in the Psalms as a rock or a fortress. He can be trusted, leaned on, and run to. If there's anything unsure in your life, you can know that it's not God who is shifting.

Jesus Christ is the same yesterday
and today and forever.
HEBREWS 13:8

No matter your past or upbringing, God is a good, good Father who loves and accepts each of His children with open arms.

You have not received a spirit of slavery leading to fear again,
but you have received a spirit of adoption as sons
by which we cry out, "Abba! Father!"
ROMANS 8:15

There *are times to be quiet and stoic. There are also times to lavish God with extravagant praise.*

Let them praise His name with dancing;
Let them sing praises to Him with timbrel and lyre.
For the Lord takes pleasure in His people;
He will beautify the afflicted ones with salvation.
Let the godly ones exult in glory;
Let them sing for joy on their beds.
PSALM 149:3-5

Spending time with God through prayer, listening, reading the Word, and many other ways can get you ready for anything that comes along.

I will meditate on Your precepts and regard Your ways.
I shall delight in Your statutes;
I shall not forget Your word.
PSALM 119:15-16

The company you keep makes a difference. Being around Jesus brings out the best in anyone. He's the very best example, and leads you along the very best path.

Keep watching and praying
that you may not enter into temptation;
the spirit is willing, but the flesh is weak.
MATTHEW 26:41

God is always good, and always works things for good. And praising Him in the midst of any storm can work wonders for your soul and attitude.

Bless the Lord, O my soul, And all that is within me,
bless His holy name. Bless the Lord, O my soul,
and forget none of His benefits.
PSALM 103:1-2

Jesus came for the broken, the lonely, the hurting, and the lost. He is drawn to the ones with sincere hearts. He loves to love those in need. And He's made us to follow in His footsteps.

Though the Lord is exalted,
yet He regards the lowly,
but the haughty He knows from afar.
PSALM 138:6

On God's team, no one is ranked by ability. Everyone is simply chosen. First. Every time. You've got the precise skillset you were designed to have, and your team needs you just as you are!

For you are a holy people to the Lord your God;
the Lord your God has chosen you
to be a people for His own possession
out of all the peoples who are on the face of the earth.
DEUTERONOMY 7:6

Stay strong, press on, and keep believing. You've got what it takes to be a kingdom-class athlete. Train hard and follow your heavenly coach's (Holy Spirit's) instructions. You've got a medal coming!

I press on toward the goal for the prize
of the upward call of God in Christ Jesus.
PHILIPPIANS 3:14

There's a peace that comes in knowing where the boundaries are, and God sets perfect boundaries. His rules are in place so that we can be free and happy in His kingdom.

Therefore we also have as our ambition,
whether at home or absent, to be pleasing to Him.
For we must all appear before the judgment seat of Christ,
so that each one may be recompensed for his deeds in the body,
according to what he has done, whether good or bad.
II CORINTHIANS 5:9-10

We are gold to our God. He works tirelessly to refine us. His hands get dirty in the mud, sifting out the junk and searching for the valuable pieces He can use. And in the end, we are His most treasured possession.

But He knows the way I take; When He has tried me,
I shall come forth as gold. My foot has held fast to His path;
I have kept His way and not turned aside.
JOB 23:10-11

Tuck yourself into the arms of the Father, and you'll never be alone. You'll be cared for richly. Your roots will go down deep into His love and stay there.

And the LORD will continually guide you,
and satisfy your desire in scorched places,
and give strength to your bones; and you will be
like a watered garden, and like a spring of water
whose waters do not fail.

ISAIAH 58:11

Grace is a miraculous thing. God provides grace for the moment, right when we need it—rarely too early, and never too late. And it always lasts as long as we need.

Those who wait for the Lord will gain new strength;
they will mount up with wings like eagles,
they will run and not get tired,
they will walk and not become weary.

ISAIAH 40:31

Some thoughts are toxic. They can actually harm us both spiritually and physically! On the other hand, hope tends to strengthen us in all ways.

Whatever is true, whatever is honorable,
whatever is right, whatever is pure, whatever is lovely,
whatever is of good repute, if there is any excellence
and if anything worthy of praise, dwell on these things.
PHILIPPIANS 4:8

We can live quiet Christian lives, calling our faith "private" or "personal"—which it most definitely is! But we can also be unashamed and open about living our faith for the world to see.

Beloved, while I was making every effort to write you
about our common salvation, I felt the necessity to write to
you appealing that you contend earnestly for the faith
which was once for all handed down to the saints.

JUDE 1:3

The easy way isn't always the best way, and the best way isn't always hard. The trick is to stay focused on Jesus and walk where He walks. If you do, you'll definitely benefit from the reward of walking well.

Suffer hardship with me, as a good soldier of Christ Jesus…
if anyone competes as an athlete, he does not win the prize
unless he competes according to the rules. The hard-working farmer
ought to be the first to receive his share of the crops.
II TIMOTHY 2:3, 5-6

God doesn't always respond in the ways we expect or want.
But anything we get from Him is right on the money.

I, the LORD, speak righteousness,
declaring things that are upright.
ISAIAH 45:19

Music can bring us closer to the Creator. Whether you can carry a tune or not, your heart is always carried to the One who created you to worship Him.

I will sing of lovingkindness and justice, to You,
O Lord, I will sing praises.
PSALM 101:1

With God all things are possible. With God, we can lean in for all sorts of amazing and miraculous things. When He says we can avoid temptation it's because He's put a failsafe in the plan—pray to, trust in, and lean on Him.

Pray that you may not enter into temptation.
LUKE 22:40

In a nutshell, God is HUGE. Just think! He holds the universe in the palm of His hand! Can you imagine the volume of love that is contained in such a vast being?

For as high as the heavens are above the earth,
so great is His lovingkindness toward those who fear Him.
As far as the east is from the west, so far has He removed
our transgressions from us.
PSALM 103:11-12

It has been said that not forgiving someone out of spite, is like cutting yourself with a knife, trying to get another person to bleed. A graphic image. But it illustrates well that the only one unforgiveness truly hurts is the person who refuses to give it.

Just as the Lord forgave you,
so also should you.
COLOSSIANS 3:13

It's been said that if the entire state of Texas were covered a foot deep in quarters, JUST ONE of those quarters would represent the odds of every single Bible prophecy of Jesus coming to light. In other words, Scripture is accurate—and Jesus is a miracle.

For I delivered to you as of first importance what I also received,
that Christ died for our sins according to the Scriptures,
and that He was buried, and that He was raised
on the third day according to the Scriptures.
I CORINTHIANS 15:3-4

God's timetable is not our own. He rarely can be moved to move. He is never early. He is never late. But He is always right on time.

The Lord is not slow about His promise,
as some count slowness, but is patient toward you,
not wishing for any to perish but for all to come to repentance.
II PETER 3:9

God loves each of us more than it makes sense. And He is the most generous giver of every good and perfect gift. So enjoy your special place in the family.

He chose us in Him before the foundation of the world,
that we would be holy and blameless before Him.
EPHESIANS 1:4

God's love is a love that just won't quit. His love is full of mercy, forgiveness, and hope. It helps erase the pain and build the future.

Love...bears all things,
believes all things, hopes all things, endures all things.
Love never fails.
I CORINTHIANS 13:4, 7-8

It may seem convenient or simpler to do whatever feels good at the moment. But there's no simpler joy than to rest in God and let Him take you on His adventures.

Enter through the narrow gate; for the gate is wide and the way is broad that leads to destruction, and there are many who enter through it. For the gate is small and the way is narrow that leads to life, and there are few who find it.

MATTHEW 7:13-14

God loves honesty, openness, and even raw feeling. He's not afraid of your tears, anger, or passion. He will just as readily dance and rejoice with you as He will to wrap you in His arms of compassion.

How can a young man keep his way pure?
By keeping it according to Your word.
With all my heart I have sought You;
do not let me wander from Your commandments.
PSALM 119:9-10

We are like sheep protected by our Shepherd. His boundaries keep us free and content in His presence.

The law of the LORD is perfect, restoring the soul; the testimony of the LORD is sure, making wise the simple. The precepts of the LORD are right, rejoicing the heart; the commandment of the LORD is pure, enlightening the eyes.

PSALM 19:7-8

It's the closeness of God that we most need when we're most overwhelmed. Only God can take us to a place of grace, where we can get through some storms.

My soul takes refuge in You; and in the shadow of Your wings I will take refuge until destruction passes by.

PSALM 57:1

Having a personal relationship with God is essential. It's also nothing to be ashamed of! Live your faith in a way that makes people notice a difference. Jesus did!

"Let him who boasts boast of this, that he understands
and knows Me, that I am the Lord who exercises lovingkindness,
justice and righteousness on earth;
for I delight in these things," declares the Lord.
JEREMIAH 9:24

Jesus is the vine and we are the branches. We have everything we need to bear much fruit in Him. We just need to stay connected.

I am the vine, you are the branches;
he who abides in Me and I in him, he bears much fruit,
for apart from Me you can do nothing.
JOHN 15:5

Knowing God, understanding Him better, and receiving His love should lead to deeper and deeper joy. The kind that can't be shaken under any circumstances.

So I commended pleasure, for there is nothing good for a man
under the sun except to eat and to drink and to be merry,
and this will stand by him in his toils throughout
the days of his life which God has given him under the sun.
ECCLESIASTES 8:15

Light *always conquers darkness, not the other way around. When the Holy Spirit lives in us, we take Him everywhere we go!*

Therefore we also have as our ambition,
whether at home or absent, to be pleasing to Him.

II CORINTHIANS 5:9

Our Shepherd knows the sounds of our desperate cries, and we instinctively know the sound of His voice.

He makes me lie down in green pastures;
He leads me beside quiet waters. He restores my soul;
He guides me in the paths of righteousness for His name's sake.
PSALM 23:2-3

Like toddlers wandering through the grass looking for the plastic eggs that Grandma has hidden, we get to enjoy and explore all the treasures of heaven when we know God.

The secret of the LORD is for those who fear Him,
and He will make them know His covenant.
PSALM 25:14

The ways of the kingdom are not like the ways of the world. God always has His eye on the faithful ones, and we can trust in His reward.

Adversity pursues sinners,
but the righteous will be rewarded with prosperity.
PROVERBS 13:21

You are a child of the King. You have access to places that many do not. The King will always make time for you, and let you sit on His lap during meetings. He is keenly interested in you!

Because he has loved Me, therefore I will deliver him;
I will set him securely on high, because he has known My name.
He will call upon Me, and I will answer him; I will be with him
in trouble; I will rescue him and honor him.

PSALM 91:14-15

Loving God means living in a way that, if your life is scrutinized,
no fault will be found.

Make it your ambition to lead a quiet life and
attend to your own business and work with your hands,
just as we commanded you, so that you will behave properly
toward outsiders and not be in any need.

I THESSALONIANS 4:11-12

FEBRUARY 28

The name of Jesus saves. He heals. He restores. He redeems. He removes obstacles and delivers victory.

The name of the LORD is a strong tower;
the righteous runs into it and is safe.
PROVERBS 18:10

It can be so hard to wait. Never mind the waiting room, long lines of traffic, or a much anticipated letter in the mail. When the waiting we're doing is on God, it can seem like forever! And how do we handle it when the answer is one we didn't want? Well, think about this. An answer from God means that the God of the universe is in relationship with us! He cares enough to hear our hearts and respond. What a beautiful thing—God's "no" may be a no, but it still shows His closeness and love.

The mind of man plans his way, but the LORD directs his steps.
PROVERBS 16:9

Need a miracle? Listen to the testimonies of others. The Lord is always up to the impossible!

With respect to the promise of God,
[Abraham] did not waver in unbelief but grew strong in faith,
giving glory to God, and being fully assured that what
God had promised, He was able also to perform.
ROMANS 4:20-21

God loves the partnership He has with His children, and sometimes He "leads from the back of the room"—by letting us learn through making decisions.

Therefore Jesus, lifting up His eyes and seeing that
a large crowd was coming to Him, said to Philip,
"Where are we to buy bread, so that these may eat?"
This He was saying to test him,
for He Himself knew what He was intending to do.
JOHN 6:5-6

God knows your every need and your every move. We, on the other hand, don't always remember God! But we have a promise. If we cry out to Him and seek Him, He will be there.

The righteous cry, and the LORD hears
and delivers them out of all their troubles.
PSALM 34:17

God does amazing things through His people. We can participate by being sensitive to what He is up to in any given moment, and being willing to let Him use us.

And when the men of that place recognized Him,
they sent word into all that surrounding district and
brought to Him all who were sick; and they implored Him
that they might just touch the fringe of His cloak;
and as many as touched it were cured.

MATTHEW 14:35-36

There are many benefits of being a child of God. We're probably not truly aware of more than five percent of His presence in our lives!

When you pass through the waters, I will be with you;
and through the rivers, they will not overflow you.
When you walk through the fire, you will not be scorched,
nor will the flame burn you. Do not fear, for I am with you;
I will bring your offspring from the east,
and gather you from the west.
ISAIAH 43:2, 5

If you're aging (as we all are), own it! You're beautiful, and your wisdom is growing day by day.

Therefore we do not lose heart,
but though our outer man is decaying,
yet our inner man is being renewed day by day.
II CORINTHIANS 4:16

The simple truth is, believe in your heart that Jesus is Lord, and confess Him with your lips. That's all it takes to be in relationship with Him. All the details will fall into place as we get to know Him.

Truly, truly, I say to you, he who hears My word,
and believes Him who sent Me, has eternal life,
and does not come into judgment,
but has passed out of death into life.

JOHN 5:24

Forgiveness is the Lord's specialty, and your sins are erased from the record when He gives it.

Nevertheless do not rejoice in this,
that the spirits are subject to you,
but rejoice that your names are recorded in heaven.
LUKE 10:20

But God is just. He always wins. And that energy it would take to fight, it can be put to use in resting in His embrace as He goes to battle for you.

The LORD will fight for you while you keep silent.
EXODUS 14:14

The Lord is the only forever-lasting Person there is. No one but He can determine your path. And He has power over the people who would manipulate you or feed on fear.

I, even I, am He who comforts you. Who are you that you are afraid of man who dies and of the son of man who is made like grass, that you have forgotten the LORD your Maker, Who stretched out the heavens and laid the foundations of the earth, that you fear continually all day long because of the fury of the oppressor, as he makes ready to destroy? But where is the fury of the oppressor?

ISAIAH 51:12-13

We are human. Imperfect, messy, gloriously beautiful humans who need the grace of God. We also sometimes need to be reminded of why we need Him.

But he said to Him, "Lord, with You I am ready
to go both to prison and to death!"
And He said, "I say to you, Peter, the rooster will not crow today
until you have denied three times that you know Me."
LUKE 22:33-34

MARCH 13

Jesus is constantly interceding for us before the throne of our Father. We can follow suit and pray for others.

Simon, Simon, behold, Satan has demanded
permission to sift you like wheat; but I have prayed for you,
that your faith may not fail; and you,
when once you have turned again,
strengthen your brothers.

LUKE 22:31-32

God's love is the best. Better even than a parent's love for their children. His heart breaks when we turn away, and He rejoices when we accept His love with open arms.

Just as the Father has loved Me,
I have also loved you; abide in My love.
JOHN 15:9

It's not your job to do life perfectly. But you can do your best to love the Lord well through it all.

Whatever you do in word or deed,
do all in the name of the Lord Jesus,
giving thanks through Him to God the Father.
COLOSSIANS 3:17

Jesus promised that the world was full of trouble. He also promised that He has overcome the world. So, do we look at the trouble, or look to the Victor? The choice is up to each of us.

Stripes that wound scour away evil,
and strokes reach the innermost parts.
PROVERBS 20:30

Jesus knows you. He knows me. And He tends to be drawn to the ones who feel most invisible, and most hungry. So lean in and show your interest. He'll certainly catch your eye.

Are not two sparrows sold for a cent?
And yet not one of them will fall to the ground apart
from your Father. So do not fear;
you are more valuable than many sparrows.
MATTHEW 10:29, 31

God's mercy is indescribable, and His tolerance so merciful. He loves our innocence, and understands our current level of maturity.

Just as a father has compassion on his children,
so the LORD has compassion on those who fear Him.
For He Himself knows our frame;
He is mindful that we are but dust.

PSALM 103:13-14

What we see now is just a glimpse of His true glory. But imagine the day when we won't have to imagine at all—we will be in His presence forever.

Bless the LORD, O my soul!
O LORD my God, You are very great;
You are clothed with splendor and majesty,
PSALM 104:1

Sometimes we end up in situations that are tailor made for our cries out to Him for help and understanding. Then when He delivers, it's so obvious where the help came from

Now, O Lord our God, I pray,
deliver us from his hand that all the kingdoms of the earth
may know that You alone, O Lord, are God.

II KINGS 19:19

"Not by might, nor by power, but by My Spirit," says the Lord (Zech. 4:6). Those who believe in Jesus have the same power that raised Him from the dead living in them.

From the days of John the Baptist
until now the kingdom of heaven suffers violence,
and violent men take it by force.
MATTHEW 11:12

With God, *your cup never runs dry. The more you pour out, the more He pours in.*

But you, beloved, building yourselves up
on your most holy faith,
praying in the Holy Spirit.
JUDE 20

MARCH 23

If you've accepted Christ, then you are a new creation. The old you, replaced. The old sin, erased. The devil's work, disgraced by Jesus.

But may it never be that I would boast,
except in the cross of our Lord Jesus Christ,
through which the world has been crucified to me,
and I to the world.
GALATIANS 6:14

God is glorious and untouchable, tender and compassionate. And by His grace, we belong right by His side.

The Law came in so that the transgression would increase; but where sin increased, grace abounded all the more.
ROMANS 5:20

God doesn't look at the situation so much as He looks at the heart. A pure and open heart can receive truth.

(God) raised us up with Him, and seated us
with Him in the heavenly places in Christ Jesus,
so that in the ages to come He might show the surpassing riches
of His grace in kindness toward us in Christ Jesus.

EPHESIANS 2:6-7

It helps so much to see what's coming. It helps to keep your eye on the one who knows where it's coming from too.

The steadfast of mind You will keep in perfect peace,
because he trusts in You.
ISAIAH 26:3

If we could understand what eternal like with the Lord will be like, we probably wouldn't think twice about the things that worry us today.

Blessed be the God and Father of our Lord Jesus Christ,
who has blessed us with every spiritual blessing
in the heavenly places in Christ.
EPHESIANS 1:3

It's countercultural and weird to some. But we, as believers, are made to stand out and shine as we lean back and rest in the Lord.

The LORD is my shepherd, I shall not want.
He makes me lie down in green pastures;
He leads me beside quiet waters. He restores my soul;
He guides me in the paths of righteousness for His name's sake.
PSALM 23:1-3

Every person on the planet is kind of like a seed. A potential-packed package that needs the right environment to grow.

For you were continually straying like sheep,
but now you have returned to the Shepherd and Guardian
of your souls.
I PETER 2:25

MARCH 30

You have a Source to turn to. You have the Answer at your fingertips. And you have the power to accomplish all things in Christ.

When I awake,
I am still with You.
PSALM 139:18

Bring your hunger to the Lord. And you will be satisfied, over and over again, for the rest of your days.

The apostles said to the Lord,
"Increase our faith!"
LUKE 17:5

God's world is a patience culture. There is so much to look forward to, far beyond anything we could dare to ask or imagine. There will be a day when His faithful people will be rewarded beyond belief.

He will set you high above all nations which He has made,
for praise, fame, and honor; and that you shall be
a consecrated people to the LORD your God,
as He has spoken.
DEUTERONOMY 26:19

The Lord looks not at the outside, but at the heart of a person. So whatever all out means to you—being sold out and willing to give whatever blesses the Lord—that is what pleases His heart.

Calling His disciples to Him, He said to them,
"Truly I say to you, this poor widow put in more than
all the contributors to the treasury;
for they all put in out of their surplus,
but she, out of her poverty, put in all she owned,
all she had to live on."

MARK 12:43-44

Restoration is beautiful. It draws two people closer together; wiser and stronger. And it showcases one of His very best gifts—hope and healing in His people.

He has made everything appropriate in its time.
He has also set eternity in their heart,
yet so that man will not find out the work
which God has done from the beginning even to the end.
ECCLESIASTES 3:11

On this side of heaven, losing loved ones is hard. But for those who love God the reward is outstanding.

Precious in the sight of the Lord
is the death of His godly ones.
PSALM 116:15

Jesus isn't looking for mindless, soulless followers who blindly say yes to every command. He wants people to see the options, good and bad—and still choose Him.

Jesus said to him, "I am the way,
and the truth, and the life;
no one comes to the Father but through Me."
JOHN 14:6

Life before Jesus can't truly be compared with life after. You were once a caterpillar, crawling and eating. Now you are a butterfly, a thing of real beauty. A new creation in Christ.

Jesus said to her, "I am the resurrection and the life;
he who believes in Me will live even if he dies,
and everyone who lives and believes in Me will never die.
Do you believe this?"
JOHN 11:25-26

The truth of Jesus is worth shouting from rooftops, to the spiritually hungry all over the world. So go! Share! Even if it's just with one person today.

For I am not ashamed of the gospel,
for it is the power of God for salvation to everyone who believes,
to the Jew first and also to the Greek.
ROMANS 1:16

Sometimes we expect God to show up in a certain way for us, but He's not there. Other times, He shows up in ways that we least expect.

The angel said to the women,
"Do not be afraid; for I know that you are looking for Jesus who has been crucified. He is not here, for He has risen, just as He said. Come, see the place where He was lying."
MATTHEW 28:5-6

It's hard to imagine a passion so deep, a loyalty so strong that a person would put his life on the line for another. But it's been done. It's the reason we have hope.

He who did not spare His own Son,
but delivered Him over for us all,
how will He not also with Him freely give us all things?
ROMANS 8:32

And whether a person likes Jesus or not, Jesus is known. A person cannot be confronted with Him and not be changed, and a person cannot forget the impact of His influence.

For we are a fragrance of Christ to God
among those who are being saved
and among those who are perishing.
II CORINTHIANS 2:15

The more we love now, the greater our treasure grows in heaven. And perhaps that gives Jesus even more to work with as He prepares your heavenly home.

In My Father's house are many dwelling places;
if it were not so, I would have told you;
for I go to prepare a place for you.
JOHN 14:2

The Lord often delivers us to the threshold of a new season. We may be given new opportunities. Or we may experience a new healing or deliverance. But the way those things play out in our lives take time and partnership with the Holy Spirit.

The LORD your God will clear away these nations before you little by little; you will not be able to put an end to them quickly, for the wild beasts would grow too numerous for you.

DEUTERONOMY 7:22

Do a spiritual checkup of your heart today. Are you willing to learn? Are you tender and soft before God? If so, there's no limit to what He can do in and through you.

Teach me, O LORD, the way of Your statutes,
and I shall observe it to the end. Give me understanding,
that I may observe Your law and keep it with all my heart.
PSALM 119:33-34

For as many as are the promises of God, in [Jesus] they are yes! (2 Cor. 1:20) The empty tomb was a sealing of the new covenant of hope and salvation.

Calling a bird of prey from the east,
the man of My purpose from a far country. Truly I have spoken;
truly I will bring it to pass. I have planned it, surely I will do it.

ISAIAH 46:11

God gives us all the resources we need to live in this world but not of it. And He delights in our partnership with Him to live out His love.

All these died in faith, without receiving the promises, but having seen them and having welcomed them from a distance, and having confessed that they were strangers and exiles on the earth. For those who say such things make it clear that they are seeking a country of their own. ...But as it is, they desire a better country, that is, a heavenly one. Therefore God is not ashamed to be called their God; for He has prepared a city for them.

HEBREWS 11:13-14, 16

The Lord loves you as family He wants to be with. He called you by name and placed you right where you belong.

For both He who sanctifies and those
who are sanctified are all from one Father;
for which reason He is not ashamed to call them brethren.

HEBREWS 2:11

If you notice behaviors or thoughts in yourself that you're not happy with, take a look at your heart with the help of Holy Spirit.

You have heard that the ancients were told, "YOU SHALL NOT COMMIT MURDER" and "Whoever commits murder shall be liable to the court." But I say to you that everyone who is angry with his brother shall be guilty before the court; and whoever says to his brother, "You good-for-nothing," shall be guilty before the supreme court; and whoever says, "You fool," shall be guilty enough to go into the fiery hell.

MATTHEW 5:21-22

Holy Spirit has chosen you as a resting place. Be aware. Sense His presence and His leading. And do all you can to help Him feel welcome with you.

Beloved, do not believe every spirit,
but test the spirits to see whether they are from God,
because many false prophets have gone out into the world.
By this you know the Spirit of God: every spirit that confesses
that Jesus Christ has come in the flesh is from God.
I JOHN 4:1-2

God gives according to His will. He knows that His will is best for us, and we don't always see the bigger picture.

This is the confidence which we have before Him, that, if we ask
anything according to His will, He hears us.
And if we know that He hears us in whatever we ask,
we know that we have the requests
which we have asked from Him.
I JOHN 5:14-15

When God says don't, He means it. That may feel defeating. But it should empower you! He never asks us to do what we can't, with His help.

Do not worry then, saying, "What will we eat?"
or "What will we drink?" or "What will we wear for clothing?"
For the Gentiles eagerly seek all these things;
for your heavenly Father knows that you need all these things.
MATTHEW 6:31-32

When you face big questions, remember this: It is not yours to worry. It is yours to trust, and receive His peace.

For I am convinced that neither death, nor life, nor angels,
nor principalities, nor things present, nor things to come,
nor powers, nor height, nor depth, nor any other created thing,
will be able to separate us from the love of God,
which is in Christ Jesus our Lord.

ROMANS 8:38-39

Some people have learned to tap into the deep joy of the Lord. They have truly experienced Nehemiah 8:10, that His joy is our strength.

A cheerful heart has a continual feast.
PROVERBS 15:15

You stand in the shadow of the King of Kings. Nothing can defeat you.

For after all it is only just for God to repay with affliction those
who afflict you...dealing out retribution to those
who do not know God and to those
who do not obey the gospel of our Lord Jesus.

II THESSALONIANS 1:6, 8

The real Lion is on your side! So be alert, and keep company with the One who has already overcome the world.

Be of sober spirit, be on the alert.
Your adversary, the devil, prowls around like a roaring lion,
seeking someone to devour.
I PETER 5:8

Jesus had every right to strut His stuff. But He washed their feet instead. The best way for you to be honored by God, is to follow His example and take the lowest position.

Pride goes before destruction,
and a haughty spirit before stumbling.
PROVERBS 16:18

Assume others have a piece of the puzzle you could benefit from, and you'll certainly become wiser for it.

Do nothing from selfishness or empty conceit,
but with humility of mind regard one another
as more important than yourselves.
PHILIPPIANS 2:3

Get and stay in tune with the Holy Spirit, your glue for remaining in the Vine.

Abide in Me, and I in you.
As the branch cannot bear fruit of itself
unless it abides in the vine,
so neither can you unless you abide in Me.
JOHN 15:4

Sin doesn't begin when a person does the wrong thing. It begins when the idea or feeling knocks on the door of her heart and she chooses to entertain it.

But each one is tempted when he is carried away and enticed by his own lust. Then when lust has conceived, it gives birth to sin; and when sin is accomplished, it brings forth death.

JAMES 1:14-15

Align yourself with the Word and with Jesus. Then be thankful when challenges come. That means you're doing good things for and with God!

Woe to you when all men speak well of you,
for their fathers used to treat
the false prophets in the same way.
LUKE 6:26

The hardest, most essential part we play happens in our minds and hearts. It is to simply believe.

Therefore they said to Him, "What shall we do,
so that we may work the works of God?"
Jesus answered and said to them,
"This is the work of God,
that you believe in Him whom He has sent."
JOHN 6:28-29

Thankfulness, encouragement, choosing not to be offended, and praying at all times, in every way, are all weapons against the devil.

The weapons of our warfare are not of the flesh,
but divinely powerful for the destruction of fortresses.

II CORINTHIANS 10:4

Only the grace of God can bring us to a place where rejoicing is an everyday, every moment way of life. But it is possible.

Rejoice in the Lord always;
again I will say, rejoice!
PHILIPPIANS 4:4

MAY 3

God's plans for you are perfect, and not one day—this side of heaven or the other—will be stolen from you.

For to me, to live is Christ and to die is gain...
But I am hard-pressed from both directions,
having the desire to depart and be with Christ,
for that is very much better.

PHILIPPIANS 1:21, 23

God's heart is for the gentle, meek, and mild. He waits for us to, with grateful hearts, open our hand and ask for what we desire.

You do not have
because you do not ask.
JAMES 4:2

Stand in awe of God, and you will be walking in the most rudimentary form of wisdom.

The fear of the LORD is the beginning of wisdom,
and the knowledge of the Holy One is understanding.
PROVERBS 9:10

The spiritual forces of this world are hard at battle. One would undermine God's plan. The other would protect it.

For our struggle is not against flesh and blood,
but against the rulers, against the powers,
against the world forces of this darkness,
against the spiritual forces of wickedness in the heavenly places.
EPHESIANS 6:12

Worship is a response to His holiness. And in order to be able to respond to something, a person needs to experience it.

But an hour is coming, and now is,
when the true worshipers will worship
the Father in spirit and truth;
for such people the Father seeks to be His worshipers.

JOHN 4:23

At this point we understand God's power in limited ways. But there will be a day when not a soul on earth is in ignorance.

But the day of the Lord will come like a thief,
in which the heavens will pass away with a roar
and the elements will be destroyed with intense heat,
and the earth and its works will be burned up.

II PETER 3:10

How we live now—and our willingness to bring others to Christ— can actually speed up the process of His coming back.

Since all these things are to be destroyed in this way,
what sort of people ought you to be in holy conduct and godliness,
looking for and hastening the coming of the day of God.
II PETER 3:11-12

We have no idea what new heaven and earth await us after the end. But we can be sure it will blow our socks off.

But according to His promise
we are looking for new heavens and a new earth,
in which righteousness dwells.
II PETER 3:13

Sometimes God's strategies seem backwards. The thing that makes the very least sense is the very right answer.

But when Jesus heard this, He said,
"This sickness is not to end in death, but for the glory of God,
so that the Son of God may be glorified by it."
Now Jesus loved Martha and her sister and Lazarus.
So when He heard that he was sick,
He then stayed two days longer in the place where He was.
JOHN 11:4-6

We're not all anointed against communicable diseases. But you do have a special calling on your life. How has God gifted you to uniquely serve others?

The Lord is my helper,
I will not be afraid.
What will man do to me?
HEBREWS 13:6

God doesn't want robots. He wants those who love Him to use their gifts for His glory.

For by Him all things were created,
both in the heavens and on earth, visible and invisible,
whether thrones or dominions or rulers or authorities—
all things have been created through Him and for Him.

COLOSSIANS 1:16

All you need is God. His presence. His love. His power. His truth. His hope. His deliverance. His salvation.

Know therefore today,
and take it to your heart, that the LORD,
He is God in heaven above and on the earth below;
there is no other.

DEUTERONOMY 4:39

But deep inside, we all need rescue. The tender, vulnerable part of us is crying out for hope and help. Movies and stories often reflect this because they reflect the deepest, loneliest parts of our hearts. We need our Savior!

The LORD also thundered in the heavens, and the Most High uttered His voice, hailstones and coals of fire. He sent out His arrows, and scattered them, and lightning flashes in abundance, and routed them...He brought me forth also into a broad place; He rescued me, because He delighted in me.

PSALM 18:13-14, 19

The breath of God is the lifeblood of our bodies. We live because He is constantly giving us breath.

The God who made the world and all things in it,
since He is Lord of heaven and earth,
does not dwell in temples made with hands;
nor is He served by human hands,
as though He needed anything,
since He Himself gives to all people life
and breath and all things.

ACTS 17:24, 25

If we let Him love us with a Father's love, God can be that source of delight to our days.

O satisfy us in the morning with Your lovingkindness,
that we may sing for joy and be glad all our days.
PSALM 90:14

The Holy Spirit lives in you. It doesn't take more than one person; just you. To do the impossible. To serve with power. To stand strong in the midst of storms.

You are from God, little children,
and have overcome them;
because greater is He who is in you
than he who is in the world.
I JOHN 4:4

You may feel too weak. Yes, you are! But His power is all you need to do miraculous things.

Now Mount Sinai was all in smoke
because the LORD descended upon it in fire;
and its smoke ascended like the smoke of a furnace,
and the whole mountain quaked violently.
When the sound of the trumpet grew louder and louder,
Moses spoke and God answered him with thunder.
EXODUS 19:18-19

We are spiritual beings in earthly bodies. But we are also seated in heavenly places with Christ.

For thus says the high and exalted One Who lives forever,
whose name is Holy, "I dwell on a high and holy place,
and also with the contrite and lowly of spirit in order
to revive the spirit of the lowly
and to revive the heart of the contrite."

ISAIAH 57:15

We may not always see the power around us, but that doesn't mean it isn't there. The Lord often reveals His plan at the very moment we need to see it or else.

The LORD of hosts is with us;
the God of Jacob is our stronghold. Selah.
PSALM 46:11

Pay close attention to the impossible opportunities that cross your path. They may be the perfect time to say no. And they may be just the way God wants to show up and amaze you.

For nothing will be impossible with God.
LUKE 1:37

Jesus has done the paying. We get to receive, if we're willing. And we get to share the awesome news of debts paid off to anyone who will listen.

For the wages of sin is death,
but the free gift of God is eternal life
in Christ Jesus our Lord.
ROMANS 6:23

There's no trickery in God. He's not the kind of leader who says one thing and does another. He always honors a pure heart.

The LORD is good to those who wait for Him,
to the person who seeks Him.
LAMENTATIONS 3:25

The world tears down. Love builds up. Hatred sows discord, and prayer strengthens.

I ask on their behalf; I do not ask on behalf of the world,
but of those whom You have given Me; for they are Yours;
and all things that are Mine are Yours,
and Yours are Mine; and I have been glorified in them.
JOHN 17:9-10

Jesus is the way to God. He is the absolute truth. He is life to all who believe. He is our doorway into heaven.

For from Him and through Him and to Him are all things.
To Him be the glory forever. Amen.
ROMANS 11:36

The Lord always delivers on His promises. We don't always know when or how, but we can believe.

For this reason I say to you,
do not be worried about your life,
as to what you will eat or what you will drink;
nor for your body, as to what you will put on.
Is not life more than food,
and the body more than clothing?
MATTHEW 6:25

Love is an endless commodity that is worth giving and giving away.

Fight the good fight of faith;
take hold of the eternal life to which you were called,
and you made the good confession
in the presence of many witnesses.

I TIMOTHY 6:12

Everything we face has kingdom value. It can all be cashed in for treasure.

Rejoice always; pray without ceasing;
in everything give thanks;
for this is God's will for you in Christ Jesus.
I THESSALONIANS 5:16-18

There's no mountain too high that the Lord can't see over it. No ocean too deep that He can't cross it to reach you. No desert too dry that He can't rain down His love and mercy.

Thus says God the LORD,
who created the heavens and stretched them out,
who spread out the earth and its offspring,
who gives breath to the people on it and spirit
to those who walk in it, "I am the LORD."
ISAIAH 42:5-6

God is love. So if you have God, you have an endless supply. The more generous you are with it, the more generous He will be with you!

Beloved, let us love one another,
for love is from God;
and everyone who loves
is born of God and knows God.

I JOHN 4:7-8

Evidence speaks volumes, and faith is strengthened on it. Seeing miracles helps a person believe.

Jesus answered and said to them, "Go and report to John what you hear and see: the BLIND RECEIVE SIGHT and the lame walk, the lepers are cleansed and the deaf hear, the dead are raised up, and the POOR HAVE THE GOSPEL PREACHED TO THEM."

MATTHEW 11:4-5

But sometimes the very best policy is to stand back and watch the Lord work, instead of getting angry. He has a plan.

(He) emptied Himself, taking the form of a bond-servant,
and being made in the likeness of men.
Being found in appearance as a man, He humbled Himself
by becoming obedient to the point of death,
even death on a cross.

PHILIPPIANS 2:7-8

The kingdom is full of reward. There's no shame—in fact, there is joy!—in wanting what the Lord has promised.

Convinced of this, I know that I will remain and continue
with you all for your progress and joy in the faith,
so that your proud confidence in me may abound
in Christ Jesus through my coming to you again.
PHILIPPIANS 1:25-26

_____

_____

_____

_____

_____

_____

_____

_____

_____

_____

_____

_____

Jesus the innocent, took on the guilt of the guilty. And that is why you are free.

He made Him who knew no sin
to be sin on our behalf,
so that we might become the righteousness
of God in Him.

II CORINTHIANS 5:21

Just as it takes deliberate effort to put pants and a top on, it takes effort to wear the virtues given us by God.

So, as those who have been chosen of God,
holy and beloved, put on a heart of compassion,
kindness, humility, gentleness and patience...
Beyond all these things put on love,
which is the perfect bond of unity.
COLOSSIANS 3:12, 14

JUNE 6

Which is harder to believe? That you are the product of a ball of gas, or the creation of a Master artist?

By faith we understand that the worlds
were prepared by the word of God,
so that what is seen was not made out of things
which are visible.
HEBREWS 11:3

There are no perfect words when praying to God, except the ones that are most genuine and sincere.

Pray, then, in this way:
"Our Father who is in heaven,
hallowed be Your name.
Your kingdom come. Your will be done,
on earth as it is in heaven."
MATTHEW 6:9-10

Even the wisest and oldest among us is a mere blip on the screen of God's eternal plan. He is the Master Architect, with a view to everything.

Do all things
without grumbling or disputing.
PHILIPPIANS 2:14

We get to represent heaven every day. We get to share the good things we know of God, and when we don't know, it's okay to say so.

Do not be hasty in word or impulsive
in thought to bring up a matter in the presence of God.
For God is in heaven and you are on the earth;
therefore let your words be few.

ECCLESIASTES 5:2

Jesus took the long road to His highest position. He started from the bottom in order to reach the lowliest of us all.

Therefore Pilate said to Him, "So You are a king?"
Jesus answered, "You say correctly that I am a king.
For this I have been born,
and for this I have come into the world,
to testify to the truth.
Everyone who is of the truth hears My voice."
JOHN 18:37

The light of Jesus can shine through the dark, even where imperfections exist.

Do all things without grumbling or disputing;
so that you will prove yourselves to be blameless and innocent,
children of God above reproach
in the midst of a crooked and perverse generation,
among whom you appear as lights in the world.
PHILIPPIANS 2:14-15

I pray for letting go and moving on. I pray for lightness and goodness. I pray for protection. I pray for all normal friends and thank you for the gentle and kind man coming my way. Thank you for my new life ☺

JUNE 12

This is your day. Right now. This moment. Whatever year you're reading this. At the time your clock currently reads. You can make a difference.

As for the days of our life,
they contain seventy years, or if due to strength,
eighty years, yet their pride is but labor and sorrow;
for soon it is gone and we fly away.
PSALM 90:10

The taste of God is amazing. Way beyond anything we could do on our own to alter our state of reality. The kingdom of heaven is real and unspeakably good.

So then do not be foolish,
but understand what the will of the Lord is.
And do not get drunk with wine, for that is dissipation,
but be filled with the Spirit.
EPHESIANS 5:17-18

The Lord *loves your willingness to give others what He has given you. And there's only good that comes from sharing a smile.*

Bright eyes gladden the heart;
good news puts fat on the bones.
PROVERBS 15:30

Mercy costs very little to give, but is a priceless gift to receive.

Blessed are the merciful,
for they shall receive mercy.

MATTHEW 5:7

You've got what it takes to be a great friend, just as Jesus is. All you need to do is watch for the chance.

If you greet only your brothers,
what more are you doing than others?
Do not even the Gentiles do the same?
MATTHEW 5:47

If you have Jesus, you have the Holy Spirit. You carry the kingdom of God with you wherever you go.

The LORD will guard your going out
and your coming in from this time forth and forever.
PSALM 121:8

Measure everything by His standard: total acceptance, absolute joy, complete fulfillment, unending love. What could possibly compare to any of that alone, never mind all together?

These things I have spoken to you
so that My joy may be in you,
and that your joy may be made full.
JOHN 15:11

Spend any time considering what would not be possible without God, and you'll be in awe again and again.

He said, "The things that are impossible
with people are possible with God."
LUKE 18:27

As our feet of faith stay firmly in place, we can dance undignified before God—like seaweed in the current.

You are to cling to the LORD your God,
as you have done to this day.
JOSHUA 23:8

You are covered. You are free. No sin was too much for Jesus, and nothing that ever happened to you that wasn't enveloped by His grace and love.

He was pierced through for our transgressions,
He was crushed for our iniquities;
the chastening for our well-being fell upon Him,
and by His scourging we are healed.

ISAIAH 53:5

Jesus has a track record for enlisting the least prepared, least expected people. Not because He's a bad judge of character, but because He's the best!

Now as they observed the confidence of Peter
and John and understood that they were uneducated
and untrained men, they were amazed,
and began to recognize them as having been with Jesus.
ACTS 4:13

The more you dwell in the present with the Lord, the more it sets you up for the future He has planned for you. The only tense you need focus on today is the present.

Jesus said to him, "No one, after putting his hand
to the plow and looking back,
is fit for the kingdom of God."
LUKE 9:62

The Lord remains our shield and protector throughout our lives. We can be strong by proxy—we're riding along on the back of our powerful Father. Nothing should shake us in His presence!

Finally, be strong in the Lord
and in the strength of His might.
EPHESIANS 6:10

If you stay connected to God, He will not let your foot slip. It takes two to hold hands...so if you grip Him, He promises to grip you back.

Now to Him who is able to keep you from stumbling,
and to make you stand in the presence of His glory blameless
with great joy, to the only God our Savior,
through Jesus Christ our Lord, be glory, majesty,
dominion and authority, before all time
and now and forever. Amen.
JUDE 24, 25

Inappropriate emotion regarding a certain source of focus may just be a sign that something other than the Lord has your attention. Don't fret—just check in with God. He'll set your feet on the right path.

For they exchanged the truth of God for a lie,
and worshiped and served the creature
rather than the Creator,
who is blessed forever. Amen.
ROMANS 1:25

Jesus has promised to come back for you, and you can carry His peace in knowing He always keeps His word.

If I go and prepare a place for you,
I will come again and receive you to Myself,
that where I am, there you may be also.
JOHN 14:3

People without the anchor of Jesus are not a good source of wisdom or example. But the Word sets your feet in a firm foundation, and sets your mind on things above.

I wait for the LORD,
my soul does wait,
and in His word do I hope.
PSALM 130:5

Emotions are always most effective when they are surrendered and submitted to God.

A gentle answer turns away wrath,
but a harsh word stirs up anger.
PROVERBS 15:1

From under the shelter of the Lord, we can go anywhere and do anything. His covering allows us to live free and confident.

He who dwells in the shelter of the Most High
will abide in the shadow of the Almighty.
I will say to the LORD, "My refuge and my fortress,
My God, in whom I trust!"

PSALM 91:1-2

....

....

....

....

....

....

....

....

....

....

....

Baptism is an act of demonstration for the world. That what Christ has done for you is real, wonderful...and worth dying for in order to live again.

Therefore we have been buried with Him
through baptism into death, so that as Christ was raised
from the dead through the glory of the Father,
so we too might walk in newness of life.
ROMANS 6:4

You could never earn what God has for you...but it is yours, no strings attached.

Do not be afraid, little flock,
for your Father has chosen gladly
to give you the kingdom.
LUKE 12:32

God's dreams and plans for us will never be seen this side of heaven.

Now to Him who is able to do far more abundantly
beyond all that we ask or think,
according to the power that works within us,
to Him be the glory.

EPHESIANS 3:20-21

Never be afraid to shine. But hide yourself in the Lord first. That way, you'll know that what shines through you is a true glimpse of heaven.

Let your light shine before men
in such a way that they may see your good works,
and glorify your Father who is in heaven.
MATTHEW 5:16

The Lord has legions of angels at His fingertips, and as His child, you are the subject of His great care and concern.

For He will give His angels charge concerning you,
to guard you in all your ways.
PSALM 91:11

The kingdom of heaven is full of those who rejoice with those who rejoice. Practicing it then will be an everyday occurrence. Practicing it now will make you a hot commodity!

We are your reason to be proud as you also are ours,
in the day of our Lord Jesus.
II CORINTHIANS 1:14

The true things of God don't have to try and convince anyone of their goodness. The closer you scrutinize, the more integrity you see in His handiwork.

Beware of the false prophets,
who come to you in sheep's clothing,
but inwardly are ravenous wolves.
You will know them by their fruits.
MATTHEW 7:15, 16

_____

_____

_____

_____

_____

_____

_____

_____

_____

_____

_____

Every effort means never giving up on the people in your life. Even
if it takes years and is full of mistakes.

With all humility and gentleness,
with patience, showing tolerance for one another in love,
being diligent to preserve the unity of the Spirit
in the bond of peace.

EPHESIANS 4:2-3

Learning to hear and understand can be challenging enough in this world! But without God's Word, the way is dark.

Your word is a lamp to my feet
and a light to my path.
PSALM 119:105

There is literally nothing beyond God's control! And there's literally nothing the two of you can't accomplish together.

Elijah was a man with a nature like ours,
and he prayed earnestly that it would not rain,
and it did not rain on the earth for three years and six months.
Then he prayed again, and the sky poured rain
and the earth produced its fruit.

JAMES 5:17-18

Children are wired to mimic and learn from the world around them. As children of God, so are we. That's why it's so important to look to the Lord for our example.

We love,
because He first loved us.
I JOHN 4:19

But what if He is the perfect example of how we should carry ourselves through the storm?

And there arose a fierce gale of wind,
and the waves were breaking over the boat so much
that the boat was already filling up.
Jesus Himself was in the stern, asleep on the cushion;
and they woke Him and said to Him,
"Teacher, do You not care that we are perishing?"

MARK 4:37-38

When God moves in ways we can't comprehend, it is best to stand in awe, and simply file His work under "Things I Won't Understand Until Heaven."

And He got up and rebuked the wind and said to the sea,
"Hush, be still." And the wind died down
and it became perfectly calm.
(The disciples) became very much afraid
and said to one another, "Who then is this,
that even the wind and the sea obey Him?"

MARK 4:39, 41

In the end, when the battle is over, the only thing remaining will be His kingdom. The enemy fights now because he still thinks he can win. But Jesus.

Who understands the power of Your anger and Your fury,
according to the fear that is due You?
PSALM 90:11

The Holy Spirit helps us to discern what is true and right from what is unhealthy and wrong. With Him, we have every resource to walk in hope and freedom.

For whatever was written in earlier times
was written for our instruction,
so that through perseverance and
the encouragement of the Scriptures we might have hope.

ROMANS 15:4

He planned you out to the last detail. There's nothing that can change who He dreamed you to be or how you can impact your world.

In Your book were all written the days
that were ordained for me,
when as yet there was not one of them.
PSALM 139:16

The Lord wants people to know Him, because once they do, they will fall in love. And loving God leads to life.

The LORD said to Gideon,
"The people who are with you are too many for Me
to give Midian into their hands,
for Israel would become boastful, saying,
'My own power has delivered me'...
I will deliver you with the 300 men...
so let all the other people go."
JUDGES 7:2, 7

JULY 18

But one of the most gentlemanly things about God is that He never forces repentance or acceptance of Him.

(If) My people who are called by My name
humble themselves and pray and seek My face
and turn from their wicked ways,
then I will hear from heaven,
will forgive their sin and will heal their land.

II CHRONICLES 7:14

If we ask, He will answer. If we believe, He will do it. If we humble ourselves, He will hear us.

If we confess our sins,
He is faithful and righteous to forgive us our sins
and to cleanse us from all unrighteousness.

I JOHN 1:9

We need knowledge and understanding. Practice succeeding, and practice failing. Direction from God and from trusted friends. We need work!

All Scripture is inspired by God and profitable for teaching,
for reproof, for correction, for training in righteousness;
so that the man of God may be adequate,
equipped for every good work.
II TIMOTHY 3:16-17

So tell the world—just start with your neighbors—what God has done in your life. It may just make history.

From that city many of the Samaritans
believed in Him because of the word of the woman who testified,
"He told me all the things that I have done."
JOHN 4:39

God has used my difficulties to
forge a relationship with him
and the church. Through the
church I have met many
great people. Wise Don. I
miss him. My close dear
friend Cheri which has
changed my life. And Erin.
A new friendship that I
believe will become a very
special relationship. God has
done everything for me
and closed doors when
I was unable to do so

JULY 22

God dares you. Just try to think of one thing that is too big and bad and ugly for Him to redeem and erase by the blood of Jesus!

But the tax collector...
was beating his breast, saying,
"God, be merciful to me, the sinner!"
I tell you, this man went to his house justified.

LUKE 18:13, 14

A tumor is not too big for God to redeem, but sometimes he doesn't work as we have prayed. Sometimes things happen and they aren't caused by God. Maybe the mercy for Cheri be the coming of a baby and a conversation with God. God may you help us with our grief and sorrow. Especially for Cheri, we saw a hawk in her backyard. It was her dad and he's waiting for her

JULY 23

Use your circumstances to strengthen those around you. Talk about the hard of it, and the beauty that most certainly comes from ashes.

Now I, Nebuchadnezzar, praise,
exalt and honor the King of heaven,
for all His works are true and His ways just,
and He is able to humble those who walk in pride.
DANIEL 4:37

These past 7 yrs have brought me to a strong relationship with God. Listening to Joyce, Joel and Keith. Going to church needing so much positivity and knowing he is the only one who is always there and will never leave.

God does not fit in a human-box any more than a housecat fits in an ant-box. Let Him show you who He is and what He can do.

Great is our Lord and abundant in strength;
His understanding is infinite.
PSALM 147:5

God is capable of anything
The Holy Ghost amazes
me every day. He puts
great thoughts and ideas
in my head

You never know, until you need it, how rich a memory bank full of Scriptural truth can be.

This book of the law shall not depart from your mouth,
but you shall meditate on it day and night,
so that you may be careful to do
according to all that is written in it;
for then you will make your way prosperous,
and then you will have success.
JOSHUA 1:8

I need to read and stop
making excuses. Will reach
out to Erin so she can
ge me pointed in the
right direction

God is many things. And one is the kindest Father you could ask for, in all the times you need Him most. He can be trusted with every piece of your heart.

Like a shepherd He will tend His flock,
in His arm He will gather the lambs and carry them in His bosom;
He will gently lead the nursing ewes.

ISAIAH 40:11

Father please lead me or more faithfully I pray I follow your lead. I have a problem with patience. I want the good life you have for me. Let me continue to learn

Serving others through a love for Jesus, makes loving the unlovable
a whole lot easier—and very rewarding.

If you love Me, you will keep My commandments.
He who has My commandments
and keeps them is the one who loves Me.
JOHN 14:15, 21

I serve Cheri but she is very
lovable a big step for me
Some of the Unlovable are
patients and I work much
harder to be kind to them.
I will try especially hard
to now that I understand

Feelings, even anger, are natural. But with the grace of God we can learn to respond instead of react.

For the anger of man does not achieve
the righteousness of God.
JAMES 1:20

Reaction is difficult for me. I always am hurt by Greg which comes out as anger. I am hurt by John's actions which show itself with sadness and not anger. What is the difference? Why is there a difference in my reaction? In both I need to respond appropriately

JULY 29

You are needed. You have something to deliver. People are waiting on you to shine your light, so that they can see the way.

Whatever is not from faith is sin.
ROMANS 14:23

If I give all my possessions to feed the poor,
and if I surrender my body to be burned, but do not have love,
it profits me nothing.
I CORINTHIANS 13:3

I try to offer Joyce to
people who are suffering
and Joyce offers you
Joyce tells me about you
and it feeds me. I want
to share you - I am outspoken
I am full of excuses and
complaints. I do not
read the Bible.
Ist waiting for the
time and now the
space - EXCUSES

Perhaps *"fandom" of this world is put into place so that we can experience the true level of what passion for the Lord could look like.*

You shall love the Lord your God
with all your heart and with all your soul
and with all your might.

DEUTERONOMY 6:5

His ways are far more attractive than religious views would have you think.

What does the LORD require of you but to do justice,
to love kindness, and to walk humbly
with your God?
MICAH 6:8

People are hungry to be seen, known, and loved for who they are. And it's no mistake that God made us to be encouragers for that very reason.

But encourage one another day after day,
as long as it is still called "Today."
HEBREWS 3:13

There's a lot we learn in the beginning that serves to get us started, but we make adjustments as we internalize the true meanings behind our actions. What God cares about is the inside—not the looks.

Whether, then, you eat or drink
or whatever you do,
do all to the glory of God.
I CORINTHIANS 10:31

The things of Jesus are truly foreign in this world. It's supposed to be that way, because we belong to a world that is way, way better!

I have given them Your word;
and the world has hated them,
because they are not of the world,
even as I am not of the world.
JOHN 17:14

The mercy of God is there for the taking, if you're willing to humbly take your place at His feet.

In repentance and rest you will be saved,
in quietness and trust is your strength.
ISAIAH 30:15

AUGUST 5

By His very life, death, and resurrection, Jesus says "So be it" to every good and perfect gift of God.

For as many as are the promises of God,
in Him they are yes; therefore also through Him
is our Amen to the glory of God through us.
II CORINTHIANS 1:20

God is the only One who sees the big picture. What may make perfect sense to you, could be in conflict with the overall purpose God has for your family or surroundings.

Come now, you who say,
"Today or tomorrow we will go to such and such a city,
and spend a year there and engage in business and make a profit."
Yet you do not know what your life will be like tomorrow.
JAMES 4:13, 14

When God says that honoring your parents will make things go well for you, you can believe Him.

Honor your father and mother...
so that it may be well with you,
and that you may live long on the earth.
EPHESIANS 6:2, 3

Knowing God's Word—and more importantly, knowing God—
will train you for things to come.

For bodily discipline is only of little profit,
but godliness is profitable for all things,
since it holds promise for the present life
and also for the life to come.
I TIMOTHY 4:8

Love means caring very much to respect who the other person is. The Lord, in His amazing love, does this for us.

Let the words of my mouth
and the meditation of my heart
be acceptable in Your sight,
O LORD, my rock and my Redeemer.
PSALM 19:14

Jesus is our ultimate goal-reacher. He has been there, right at the beginning where we began. And now He sits victoriously in heaven!

Fixing our eyes on Jesus,
the author and perfecter of faith,
who for the joy set before Him endured the cross,
despising the shame, and has sat down
at the right hand of the throne of God.
HEBREWS 12:2

The Holy Spirit is our trailblazer through life. Without Him, people are wandering and confused. With Him, it may not be easy— but it will definitely be safer and more sure.

You will make known to me the path of life;
in Your presence is fullness of joy;
in Your right hand there are pleasures forever.
PSALM 16:11

The treasure troves of heaven are rich with mounds of wisdom; endless supplies of miracles and gifts.

Oh, the depth of the riches both of the wisdom
and knowledge of God!
How unsearchable are His judgments
and unfathomable His ways!
ROMANS 11:33

Hearing the Holy Spirit takes supreme focus, and a desire to actually locate the sound of His voice. It takes a willingness to release all other distractions and listen beyond the static noises of the world.

After the wind an earthquake,
but the LORD was not in the earthquake.
After the earthquake a fire, but the LORD was not in the fire;
and after the fire a sound of a gentle blowing.

I KINGS 19:11, 12

Knowing is a verb. Which means, knowing is an action. It is a deliberate act on our behalf to do something.

Cease striving
and know that I am God.
PSALM 46:10

One of the best ways to be a good friend is to be the kind of friend you yourself would like to have.

But everyone must be quick to hear,
slow to speak and slow to anger.
JAMES 1:19

The end is not the goal for everyday life. The journey is! Where you are today is where God wants you.

For I am confident of this very thing,
that He who began a good work in you will
perfect it until the day of Christ Jesus.
PHILIPPIANS 1:6

AUGUST 17

We get discouraged if we pray for one person and that person does not get well. But what if we pray for 100? If one gets healed from cancer, is that worth it?

Ask, and it will be given to you;
seek, and you will find;
knock, and it will be opened to you.
MATTHEW 7:7

God knew where He was headed when He knitted you together. He had your whole life dreamed up.

You formed my inward parts;
You wove me in my mother's womb.
PSALM 139:13

We do not fight alone. In fact, we are part of a great army of Saints, surrounded by the Lord's protection.

You have enclosed me behind and before,
and laid Your hand upon me.
Such knowledge is too wonderful for me;
it is too high, I cannot attain to it.

PSALM 139:5-6

Leaving *a hard situation without dealing with the root cause won't solve the problem. That problem will follow you if it originates inside. But the Lord follows you too.*

If I take the wings of the dawn,
If I dwell in the remotest part of the sea,
even there Your hand will lead me,
And Your right hand will lay hold of me.
PSALM 139:9-10

We who have God as our Father can jump up and cheer too. What we have is the opportunity for so much growth, love, fun, and adventure in life.

Let all who take refuge in You be glad,
let them ever sing for joy;
and may You shelter them,
that those who love Your name may exult in You.
PSALM 5:11

There are enough chances in life to figure things out on our own. But when we have a wise companion with us, it's a great idea to let them lead us.

It is better to listen to the rebuke of a wise man
than for one to listen to the song of fools.
ECCLESIASTES 7:5

AUGUST 23

*With God, we have the trustworthy loyalty of calling His name,
and knowing He is right there with us.*

The LORD is near to all who call upon Him,
to all who call upon Him in truth.
PSALM 145:18

Jesus said that loving the Lord your God with all our heart, soul, and mind (Lk. 10:27) is the greatest command we have.

Now for this very reason also, applying all diligence,
in your faith supply moral excellence,
and in your moral excellence, knowledge.

II PETER 1:5

When Jesus died, the veil was torn—our separation from the Father was no longer an issue. We were welcomed into His presence by grace alone.

Be diligent to present yourself approved to God
as a workman who does not need to be ashamed,
accurately handling the word of truth.
II TIMOTHY 2:15

Stay in tune. Be God's partner. Pay attention to the things that stir your heart in a special way. Then go out in joy, and serve. He will show you the way.

For we are His workmanship,
created in Christ Jesus for good works,
which God prepared beforehand
so that we would walk in them.
EPHESIANS 2:10

The ways of the Spirit are specific and recognizable. Anyone who doesn't follow His lead will be out of step with the kingdom of God.

If we live by the Spirit,
let us also walk by the Spirit.
GALATIANS 5:25

God loves to delight those who delight in Him.

Delight yourself in the Lord;
and He will give you the desires of your heart.
PSALM 37:4

Define success with the Holy Spirit, not according to the world's standards—and you'll live a much happier, more satisfied life.

May He grant you your heart's desire
And fulfill all your counsel!
PSALM 20:4

Maybe that thing you started is exactly the field He wanted to use to grow your patience and endurance.

The end of a matter
is better than its beginning;
Patience of spirit
is better than haughtiness of spirit.
ECCLESIASTES 7:8

Faith *is the evidence of things not seen. It's great to know what's coming. But it is grand to take steps forward, believing God, trusting in His promises.*

For we walk by faith,
not by sight.
II CORINTHIANS 5:7

But with Jesus, records of sin are erased. We start with a clean slate, washed pure and white and clean.

If You, LORD, should mark iniquities,
O Lord, who could stand?
But there is forgiveness with You,
that You may be feared.
PSALM 130:3-4

God is love. Every characteristic that can be applied to love, can be applied to God.

Love is patient, love is kind and is not jealous;
love does not brag and is not arrogant,
does not act unbecomingly;
it does not seek its own, is not provoked,
does not take into account a wrong suffered.

I CORINTHIANS 13:4-5

When we're brimming with hope and love, our kindness tends to overflow from our hearts into the world around us.

Jesus answered and said to him,
"If anyone loves Me, he will keep My word;
and My Father will love him,
and We will come to him
and make Our abode with him."

JOHN 14:23

Jesus is a loving leader boss. He's a perfect example, a servant, a helper and a prayer warrior on your behalf.

For the Son of Man is going to come
in the glory of His Father with His angels,
and will then repay every man
according to his deeds.

MATTHEW 16:27

There is no one but God. No name other than Jesus. And no other promise for hope, joy, peace, fulfilment and freedom.

And there is salvation in no one else;
for there is no other name under heaven that
has been given among men by which we must be saved.

ACTS 4:12

God knows us well enough not to be surprised or offended by our emotions and struggles. But in the end, the reward will be for those who profess Jesus and follows His leading.

Not everyone who says to Me,
"Lord, Lord," will enter the kingdom of heaven,
but he who does the will of My Father
who is in heaven will enter.
MATTHEW 7:21

Try going on a treasure hunt. One through the Bible, to discover what it looks like to love the Lord with all your mind.

And He said to him,
"You shall love the Lord your God
with all your heart, and with all your soul,
and with all your mind."
MATTHEW 22:37

The cross was a violent act. Nothing about it was tame or easy. But it wasn't pointed at us. It happened for us.

For God has not destined us for wrath,
but for obtaining salvation through our Lord Jesus Christ,
who died for us, so that whether we are awake or asleep,
we will live together with Him. Therefore encourage one another
and build up one another, just as you also are doing.

1 THESSALONIANS 5:9-11

You have an advocate for you, and His name is Jesus.

To this end also we pray for you always,
that our God will count you worthy of your calling,
and fulfill every desire for goodness
and the work of faith with power.

II THESSALONIANS 1:11

God's love is what warms us from the inside out. His character of love is what allows us to feel loved and give love.

Your kingdom is an everlasting kingdom,
and Your dominion endures throughout all generations.
PSALM 145:13

Jesus had no secret stash of superhero strength. However, He did
have a supernatural relationship of grace with His Father.

For we do not have a high priest
who cannot sympathize with our weaknesses,
but One who has been tempted in all things as we are,
yet without sin.
HEBREWS 4:15

We are the fragrance of Christ. Everywhere we go, we give off the scent of Jesus.

But thanks be to God,
who always leads us in triumph in Christ,
and manifests through us the sweet aroma
of the knowledge of Him in every place.

II CORINTHIANS 2:14

Mercy is receiving a reward that directly opposes what our actions deserve.

Blessed be the God and Father of our Lord Jesus Christ,
who according to His great mercy
has caused us to be born again to a living hope
through the resurrection of Jesus Christ
from the dead.

I PETER 1:3

Think of the new covenant of Jesus' blood—grace and mercy—as a fulfillment of the old covenant of Law.

When you were dead in your transgressions
and the uncircumcision of your flesh,
He made you alive together with Him,
having forgiven us all our transgressions.

COLOSSIANS 2:13-14

Forgiveness is warfare—to protect your own heart from bitterness, and to protect your relationship with the one who hurt you.

Then Peter came and said to Him,
"Lord, how often shall my brother sin against me
and I forgive him? Up to seven times?"
Jesus said to him, "I do not say to you,
up to seven times,
but up to seventy times seven."
MATTHEW 18:21-22

As much as your Father forgives you, loves you, and shows you mercy—receive it, and offer that same grace to yourself.

For the good that I want,
I do not do, but I practice
the very evil that I do not want.

ROMANS 7:19

One of the saddest sights is a Christian who is still enslaved to his past. Because of Jesus, power was given to you to serve God in the world. You can break free!

I have been crucified with Christ;
and it is no longer I who live, but Christ lives in me;
and the life which I now live in the flesh
I live by faith in the Son of God,
who loved me and gave Himself up for me.

GALATIANS 2:20

The very best thing to do, when you've been offended,
is to forgive.

Be angry, and yet do not sin;
do not let the sun go down on your anger,
and do not give the devil an opportunity.
EPHESIANS 4:26-27

There's nothing wrong with making plans to live wisely. But as far as where our trust lies, that only belongs in one place.

My soul, wait in silence for God only,
for my hope is from Him.
He only is my rock and my salvation,
My stronghold; I shall not be shaken.
PSALM 62:5-6

Trust Him, seek Him, follow Him even through the valleys—and Jehovah Jireh will lead you to abundant places!

Then the Lord said to Moses,
"Behold, I will rain bread from heaven for you;
and the people shall go out and
gather a day's portion every day, that I may test them,
whether or not they will walk in My instruction."

EXODUS 16:4

Withdraw into the arms of God, and you will find a peace that passes understanding.

But you, when you pray,
go into your inner room, close your door
and pray to your Father who is in secret,
and your Father who sees
what is done in secret will reward you.

MATTHEW 6:6

In the face of trouble, there a wise One who leans in and whispers peace. Be still, and know that He is God.

This poor man cried,
and the Lord heard him
and saved him out of all his troubles.
PSALM 34:6

What help do you need from our limitless God today?

And my God will supply
all your needs
according to His riches in glory
in Christ Jesus.

PHILIPPIANS 4:19

People have searched for answers other than God. But there is only One. No other god can hold a candle to the Alpha and Omega.

For from days of old they have not heard
or perceived by ear, nor has the eye seen
a God besides You, who acts in behalf
of the one who waits for Him.

ISAIAH 64:4

God isn't asking you to solve life. He's asking you to focus on His face, and just do the next thing.

So do not worry about tomorrow;
for tomorrow will care for itself.
Each day has enough trouble of its own.
MATTHEW 6:34

The very definition of faith includes the requirement that you
not be able to see into the future.

Declaring the end from the beginning,
and from ancient times things which have not been done,
Saying, "My purpose will be established,
and I will accomplish all My good pleasure."
ISAIAH 46:10

To be forgiven. Offenses forgotten. A do-over every time you ask. A clean slate and a fresh start. New mercy today that didn't exist last night.

I, even I, am the one who wipes out
your transgressions for My own sake,
and I will not remember your sins.
ISAIAH 43:25

God's grace is truly overwhelming, and miracles are not outdated.
Keep praying, keep working, and keep believing.

As sin reigned in death,
even so grace would reign through righteousness
to eternal life through Jesus Christ our Lord.
ROMANS 5:21

Discipline lasts for a short season; shorter if you're a fast learner. The freedom and joy of maturity will last forever.

Who is a God like You,
who pardons iniquity and passes over the rebellious act
of the remnant of His possession?
He does not retain His anger forever,
because He delights in unchanging love.

MICAH 7:18

Do you want to be seen for your work, or do you enjoy going unnoticed? It matters little in the end: but true sacrifice is seen by God, and that's the thing to delight in.

Greater love has no one than this,
that one lay down his life for his friends.
JOHN 15:13

Stay in tune with the Father, and then pay attention to the people who cross your path. You may have just the touch they need to be well.

While the sun was setting,
all those who had any who were sick with various diseases
brought them to Him;
and laying His hands on each one of them,
He was healing them.

LUKE 4:40

Every experience you have can lead to the wisdom of God, if you
ask for it and keep your eyes open.

The fear of the LORD is the beginning of wisdom;
a good understanding have all those
who do His commandments;
His praise endures forever.
PSALM 111:10

A life in God's hands leads to the most profound peace, a peace unlike the kind the world gives.

But godliness actually is a means of great gain
when accompanied by contentment.
I TIMOTHY 6:6

God protects us from knowing some challenges ahead, because He knows we have a strong instinct for self-protection.

Whatever you do, do your work heartily,
as for the Lord rather than for men,
knowing that from the Lord you will receive
the reward of the inheritance.
It is the Lord Christ whom you serve.
COLOSSIANS 3:23-24

Prayer only works when we go to Him. The same rules apply as with people: Be honest, listen well, and have a humble heart.

In the same way the Spirit also helps our weakness;
for we do not know how to pray as we should,
but the Spirit Himself intercedes for us
with groanings too deep for words.
ROMANS 8:26

The Spirit talks to the Father about you. He builds you up and represents you well!

He who searches the hearts
knows what the mind of the Spirit is,
because He intercedes for the saints
according to the will of God.
ROMANS 8:27

God is not in the ignoring needs business. The fact that you call on Him is a delight to His heart.

Call upon Me in the day of trouble;
I shall rescue you, and you will honor Me.
PSALM 50:15

At the core, we are all sheep. We all flock together. We all follow the same Shepherd.

How precious is Your lovingkindness, O God!
And the children of men take refuge
in the shadow of Your wings.
They drink their fill of the abundance of Your house;
and You give them to drink of the river of Your delights.

PSALM 36:7-8

Nothing escapes the Lord's sight, and He will work all things for His glory. Just hang tight and watch Him do His thing.

Be gracious to me, O God, according to Your lovingkindness;
according to the greatness of Your compassion
blot out my transgressions....
Against You, You only, I have sinned and done
what is evil in Your sight, so that You are justified
when You speak and blameless when You judge.

PSALM 51:1, 4

You are desperately needed—your laughter, spunk, tenderness, compassion, and whatever gifts He has given you. Not a moment of your life is wasted, in His book.

So teach us to number our days,
that we may present to You a heart of wisdom.
PSALM 90:12

Learn from the apostle Paul, who took time to write "Keep on doing what you're doing," and go encourage someone today.

But you are to cling to the LORD your God,
as you have done to this day.
JOSHUA 23:8

God is keenly aware of every single detail of every single life. He's the only one who really, truly gets you!

But the very hairs of your head
are all numbered.
MATTHEW 10:30

Remembering what God has done can build faith that He will do it again. *Listening to others' stories can strengthen your own.*

The LORD appeared to him from afar, saying,
"I have loved you with an everlasting love;
therefore I have drawn you with lovingkindness."
JEREMIAH 31:3

Good work of the Lord in the lives of the people around you, may just be the wake of His presence.

Surely goodness and lovingkindness
will follow me all the days of my life,
and I will dwell in the house of the Lord forever.
PSALM 23:6

Jesus knows rejection on a deeper level, and in more brutal ways than we will ever experience in our lifetime. But He also received the King's reward in the end.

For consider Him who has endured such hostility
by sinners against Himself,
so that you will not grow weary and lose heart.
HEBREWS 12:3

God knew us even before we were in the womb (Jer. 1:5)! He has been speaking to us since the very beginning.

My sheep hear My voice,
and I know them,
and they follow Me.
JOHN 10:27

The Bible says that the Spirit calls us and leads us. He never sends us on ahead to a place He hasn't been.

To him the doorkeeper opens, and the sheep hear his voice,
and he calls his own sheep by name and leads them out.
When he puts forth all his own, he goes ahead of them,
and the sheep follow him because they know his voice.
JOHN 10:3-4

God needs no tough, hardened heart from you. He invites you to be raw and vulnerable. In fact, that's when He does His best work.

Look at the birds of the air, that they do not sow,
nor reap nor gather into barns,
and yet your heavenly Father feeds them.
Are you not worth much more than they?
MATTHEW 6:26

We can take the wheel and be responsible for all of the road hazards and safe driving, or we can enjoy the scenery and go where He takes us.

And do not be conformed to this world,
but be transformed by the renewing of your mind,
so that you may prove what the will of God is,
that which is good and acceptable and perfect.
ROMANS 12:2

Asking questions isn't doubting God, if in asking you know He has the answer.

The Lord will accomplish what concerns me;
Your lovingkindness, O Lord, is everlasting;
do not forsake the works of Your hands.
PSALM 138:8

It's easy to think of God as big and strong and powerful and Holy, which He certainly is. But He also has a mother's touch for our gentle, childlike heart.

The LORD your God is in your midst, a victorious warrior.
He will exult over you with joy,
He will be quiet in His love,
He will rejoice over you with shouts of joy.
ZEPHANIAH 3:17

The Lord watches for His faithful players. He carries the refreshment we need, and eagerly fills our cup when we need it.

For the eyes of the LORD move to and fro
throughout the earth that He may strongly support
those whose heart is completely His.

II CHRONICLES 16:9

The Holy Spirit will always stir up the soil of faith when the time is right.

For I am mindful of the sincere faith within you,
which first dwelt in your grandmother Lois
and your mother Eunice,
and I am sure that it is in you as well.

II TIMOTHY 1:5

But the only thing to be sure of is Jesus, the One who never changes. Any other plumb line has a shaky foundation or a crooked board here and there.

Jesus Christ is the same yesterday
and today and forever.
HEBREWS 13:8

We live in a world that will disappear. But that's not a threat; it's a promise!

For here we do not have a lasting city,
but we are seeking the city which is to come.
HEBREWS 13:14

What if your joy ran so deep that you just couldn't help brightening any room you entered?

For it is You who blesses the righteous man, O LORD,
You surround him with favor as with a shield.
PSALM 5:12

When it's His plan and you're willing, you simply cannot fail.

I can do all things
through Him who strengthens me.
PHILIPPIANS 4:13

We need the real food of God to stay spiritually strong.

Why do you spend money for what is not bread,
and your wages for what does not satisfy?
Listen carefully to Me, and eat what is good,
and delight yourself in abundance.
Incline your ear and come to Me.
Listen, that you may live.

ISAIAH 55:2-3

The kingdom of God doesn't need help. But God does want you to help He's given you a role to play for His glory, and your good.

And He was saying,
"The kingdom of God is like a man
who casts seed upon the soil;
and he goes to bed at night and gets up by day,
and the seed sprouts and grows—
how, he himself does not know.

MARK 4:26-27

We've all needed the precise and life-saving help of the holy Healer.

Moreover, I will give you a new heart
and put a new spirit within you;
and I will remove the heart of stone from your flesh
and give you a heart of flesh.
I will put My Spirit within you and cause you
to walk in My statutes, and you will be careful
to observe My ordinances.

EZEKIEL 36:26-27

The crown of life comes to those who simply don't give up.

Blessed is a man who perseveres under trial;
for once he has been approved,
he will receive the crown of life
which the Lord has promised to those who love Him.

JAMES 1:12

This ministry requires no special training. It simply requires a person to...well, be present. To show up. It's the kind of love that says, "Whatever you need, I'm here for you."

Therefore I urge you, brethren,
by the mercies of God, to present your bodies
a living and holy sacrifice, acceptable to God,
which is your spiritual service of worship.
ROMANS 12:1

Jesus jumped in before conditions were perfect. And His actions are what made the shift for us, from certain death to eternal life.

God demonstrates
His own love toward us,
in that while we were yet sinners,
Christ died for us.
ROMANS 5:8

Casting cares on the Lord can also mean giving Him whatever shreds of good there are, and allowing Him to work them together for good (Rom. 8:28).

Cast your burden upon the LORD
and He will sustain you;
He will never allow the righteous
to be shaken.

PSALM 55:22

Our experiences serve to teach and train us about God and His character. Our experiences can also minister to others who go through similar pain.

Blessed be the God and Father of our Lord Jesus Christ,
the Father of mercies and God of all comfort, who comforts us
in all our affliction so that we will be able
to comfort those who are in any affliction with
the comfort with which we ourselves are comforted by God.

II CORINTHIANS 1:3-4

Even if we haven't seen that particular miracle in our own lives before, we can be sure God can do it.

Let us hold fast the confession
of our hope without wavering,
for He who promised is faithful.
HEBREWS 10:23

Offenses are "O"-shaped fence around a person's heart, keeping them from the fullness of joy.

So he got up and came to his father.
But while he was still a long way off,
his father saw him and felt compassion for him,
and ran and embraced him and kissed him.

LUKE 15:20

He has hand-picked each of us, equipped us abundantly, and commissioned us to bring the light of hope!

For He rescued us from the domain of darkness,
and transferred us to the kingdom
of His beloved Son, in whom we have redemption,
the forgiveness of sins.

COLOSSIANS 1:13-14

There is One who is always working on your behalf. You may not see what He's up to, but you can know He's in your favor.

But now, thus says the LORD, your Creator, O Jacob,
and He who formed you, O Israel,
"Do not fear, for I have redeemed you;
I have called you by name; you are Mine!"

ISAIAH 43:1

Integrity means acting the same when no one is looking, as you would when all eyes are on you.

Keep your behavior excellent among the Gentiles,
so that in the thing in which they slander you as evildoers,
they may because of your good deeds,
as they observe them,
glorify God in the day of visitation.

I PETER 2:12

The Lord invites us to come see things from His point of view. All we need to do is ask.

Therefore if you have been raised up with Christ,
keep seeking the things above, where Christ is,
seated at the right hand of God.
COLOSSIANS 3:1

If God only gave you what you needed for survival, then what would you have to give away? Loving others is a necessary part of your life!

He humbled you and let you be hungry,
and fed you with manna which you did not know,
nor did your fathers know, that He might make you understand
that man does not live by bread alone, but man lives
by everything that proceeds out of the mouth of the Lord.

DEUTERONOMY 8:3

There will be a day when all of us experience freedom like we've never known. Every sorrow, every injustice, every hurt will be swallowed up by the victory of Jesus.

For the Lord Himself will descend from heaven with a shout,
with the voice of the archangel and with the trumpet of God,
and the dead in Christ will rise first.
1 THESSALONIANS 4:16

Being still and quiet in nature is a powerful way to see God at work.

The heavens are telling of the glory of God;
and their expanse is declaring the work of His hands.
Day to day pours forth speech,
and night to night reveals knowledge.

PSALM 19:1-2

If you learn to place your expectation in God alone—believing that He is good, and that He will do good—you will not be disappointed.

In the morning, O LORD,
You will hear my voice;
in the morning I will order my prayer to You
and eagerly watch.
PSALM 5:3

God only asks us to do what we can. He will do what we can't.

Wait for the LORD;
be strong and let your heart take courage;
yes, wait for the LORD.
PSALM 27:14

A parent who invests in their child by investing in God's lead, blesses His heart.

Let us not lose heart in doing good,
for in due time we will reap
if we do not grow weary.
GALATIANS 6:9

Our weapons of grace and forgiveness can cut the devil to the heart, every time. So use them often!

So then, while we have opportunity,
let us do good to all people,
and especially to those
who are of the household of the faith.
GALATIANS 6:10

Blessings have a way of hiding until you look for them.

With good will render service,
as to the Lord, and not to men,
knowing that whatever good thing each one does,
this he will receive back from the Lord,
whether slave or free.

EPHESIANS 6:7-8

We may not know exactly what's coming, but we can trust it's going to be good.

"For I know the plans that I have for you,"
declares the LORD,
"plans for welfare and not for calamity
to give you a future and a hope."
JEREMIAH 29:11

Man in his power, is hardly the tiniest fraction of God in His.

Some boast in chariots
and some in horses,
but we will boast
in the name of the LORD, our God.
PSALM 20:7

God's answers often come through experience. Because by knowing instead of just hearing, we get all the feelings and understanding that can come no other way.

Call to Me and I will answer you,
and I will tell you great and mighty things,
which you do not know.
JEREMIAH 33:3

God's Word is even more reliable than a homing pigeon. What He sends out always serves its purpose. It never returns empty-handed.

So will My word be which goes forth from My mouth;
it will not return to Me empty,
without accomplishing what I desire,
And without succeeding in the matter for which I sent it.
ISAIAH 55:11

If you've truly experienced God. on a personal level, you know you can never go back.

He saved us, not on the basis of deeds
which we have done in righteousness,
but according to His mercy,
by the washing of regeneration
and renewing by the Holy Spirit,
whom He poured out upon us richly
through Jesus Christ our Savior.
TITUS 3:5-6

What the world thinks is far inferior to the tune of the Lord's delight in our ears and hearts.

Let them shout for joy and rejoice,
who favor my vindication;
and let them say continually,
"The Lord be magnified,
who delights in the prosperity of His servant."

PSALM 35:27

Who and what God is will keep us casting our crowns and falling on our faces in utter joy for the rest of our eternal lives.

Then I looked, and I heard the voice of many angels
around the throne and the living creatures and the elders;
and the number of them was myriads of myriads,
and thousands of thousands.

REVELATION 5:11-12

God knows the world is too unstable for us to trust in anything or anyone but Him. He wants our whole heart, because He is the only One who can shelter it well.

For where your treasure is,
there your heart will be also.
LUKE 12:34

Any gods created by people are just...wood. Or metal. Or figments of imagination. But nothing—no one—can hold a candle to the King of Kings.

Thus says the LORD, the King of Israel and his Redeemer,
the LORD of hosts: "I am the first and I am the last,
and there is no God besides Me...
Do not tremble and do not be afraid;
have I not long since announced it to you and declared it?
And you are My witnesses. Is there any God besides Me,
or is there any other Rock? I know of none."
ISAIAH 44:6, 8

Legacy is valuable in the kingdom of heaven. Any person who sets the tone for the ones coming after them, is setting their family up for great blessing.

The memory of the righteous is blessed.

PROVERBS 10:7

Jesus sent the Spirit of God as a gift of Presence. His presence is comfort, guidance, wisdom, and a deposit for the infinite treasures of heaven.

I am with you always,
even to the end of the age.
MATTHEW 28:20

When the time is right, each of us is welcomed with the lavishing kisses of His glorious inheritance in heaven.

Then the King will say to those on His right,
"Come, you who are blessed of My Father,
inherit the kingdom prepared for you
from the foundation of the world."

MATTHEW 25:34

DECEMBER 1

Jesus doesn't want us to carry anything that could harm us or weigh us down. But He Himself can handle everything that concerns us!

Therefore humble yourselves
under the mighty hand of God,
that He may exalt you at the proper time,
casting all your anxiety on Him,
because He cares for you.
I PETER 5:6-7

Nothing is too little for Him. Nothing is too big for Him. Because all of the things pertain to you...and you, my friend, are His favorite.

These things I have spoken to you,
so that in Me you may have peace.
In the world you have tribulation, but take courage;
I have overcome the world.
JOHN 16:33

God waits until we're ready. But when we move, He moves.

Draw near to God
and He will draw near to you.
JAMES 4:8

Our heart status matters more than our pocket status. Are we acting out of love, or with respect to what we think we can spare?

Give, and it will be given to you.
They will pour into your lap a good measure—
pressed down, shaken together, and running over.
For by your standard of measure
it will be measured to you in return.

LUKE 6:38

You can't. But God can. All it takes is faith, patience, and connection to His heart.

And He said to them,
"Because of the littleness of your faith;
for truly I say to you,
if you have faith the size of a mustard seed,
you will say to this mountain,
'Move from here to there,' and it will move;
and nothing will be impossible to you."
MATTHEW 17:20

Check your heart and make sure your posture before God is open to possibilities. His plan for success probably won't look much like what you think it should.

The LORD said to him (Moses),
"Who has made man's mouth? Or who makes him mute or deaf,
or seeing or blind? Is it not I, the LORD?
Now then go, and I, even I, will be with your mouth,
and teach you what you are to say."
EXODUS 4:11-12

When confronted with Jesus, a person will either be drawn in or push away. God is divisive—and that's what makes Him trustworthy, unchanging, and true.

For the word of God is living and active
and sharper than any two-edged sword,
and piercing as far as the division of soul and spirit,
of both joints and marrow, and able to judge
the thoughts and intentions of the heart.

HEBREWS 4:12

The more we seek God and pray, the more we'll be in line with His plans for our future.

For the Scripture says to Pharaoh,
"FOR THIS VERY PURPOSE I RAISED YOU UP,
TO DEMONSTRATE MY POWER IN YOU,
AND THAT MY NAME MIGHT BE PROCLAIMED
THROUGHOUT THE WHOLE EARTH."
ROMANS 9:17

The power of our words only belongs in one place: in the hands of the Holy Spirit, who can help guide and guard our lips.

Set a guard, O LORD, over my mouth;
keep watch over the door of my lips.
PSALM 141:3

God is not into religion. He has laws in place, but He is intent on our success. So life with the Lord is an open Book test.

The LORD is compassionate and gracious,
slow to anger and abounding in lovingkindness...
He has not dealt with us according to our sins,
nor rewarded us according to our iniquities.

PSALM 103:8, 10

God thinks about us all the time. He chooses His gifts according to what He knows will bless our hearts.

Every good thing given and every perfect gift is from above,
coming down from the Father of lights,
with whom there is no variation or shifting shadow.
JAMES 1:17

DECEMBER 12

There's no shortcut to maturity in Christ. Persevering with God comes with its own kind of unique reward—and it is so worth the work.

And let endurance have its perfect result,
so that you may be perfect and complete,
lacking in nothing.
JAMES 1:4

DECEMBER 13

Yes, people make life more complicated. But it's the simplest thing in the world to love Jesus among others who are loving Him too.

Let us consider how to stimulate one another to love
and good deeds, not forsaking our own assembling together,
as is the habit of some, but encouraging one another;
and all the more as you see the day drawing near.
HEBREWS 10:24-25

Not much can shake the wisest of people, because they've been shaken before and still remain standing.

A man's discretion makes him slow to anger,
and it is his glory to overlook a transgression.
PROVERBS 19:11

DECEMBER 15

Her desperation never left. But neither did He. It was a training exercise called *How to Cling to the Rock*.

God is our refuge and strength,
a very present help in trouble.

PSALM 46:1

If you trust Me, you'll feel a major difference. You'll learn over time what a true Partner and Friend I am to those who love Me.

Thus says the LORD, "Cursed is the man who trusts
in mankind and makes flesh his strength,
and whose heart turns away from the LORD...
Blessed is the man who trusts in the LORD
and whose trust is the LORD."

JEREMIAH 17:5, 7

DECEMBER 17

There will be a day when our God will take His place before the whole earth, and rule in all His glorious majesty.

And I heard a loud voice from the throne, saying,
"Behold, the tabernacle of God is among men,
and He will dwell among them, and they shall be His people,
and God Himself will be among them."

REVELATION 21:3

You'll always be able to point out flaws if you look for them. It's best to choose to believe: You are a masterpiece.

I will give thanks to You,
for I am fearfully and wonderfully made;
wonderful are Your works,
and my soul knows it very well.

PSALM 139:14

The next time you feel deprived of something, ask the Lord if want you want is good in His eyes. Then allow Him to lead you to the good things He's stored up for you today!

They who seek the LORD
shall not be in want of any good thing.

PSALM 34:10

It's easy to see what's seeable, and that's where a person's mind dwells. But the mind of God searches the heart of mankind—in places no human can see.

But the LORD said to Samuel,
"Do not look at his appearance or
at the height of his stature, because I have rejected him;
for God sees not as man sees,
for man looks at the outward appearance,
but the LORD looks at the heart."

I SAMUEL 16:7

God is Creator. He created, He creates, and He will create—even today, even right now.

In the beginning
God created the heavens and the earth.

GENESIS 1:1

As a servant in God's house you can believe—
you will be taken care of.

You whom I have taken from the ends of the earth,
and called from its remotest parts and said to you,
"You are My servant,
I have chosen you and not rejected you."
ISAIAH 41:9-10

A prince's friendships are open and fruitful.
He serves more than he expects.

Jude, a bond-servant of Jesus Christ,
and brother of James,
to those who are the called,
beloved in God the Father,
and kept for Jesus Christ:
may mercy and peace
and love be multiplied to you.

JUDE 1-2

Tonight is the time to set aside the hustle and bustle. To release the "undones" and welcome the moments of peace and reflection and joy.

Looking for the blessed hope
and the appearing of the glory
of our great God and Savior, Christ Jesus.

TITUS 2:13

Jesus is always the beginning of the journey, whether you've known Him forever or not at all. Anyone who takes His outreached hand is walking in the very best way.

For God so loved the world,
that He gave His only begotten Son,
that whoever believes in Him shall not perish,
but have eternal life.
JOHN 3:16

DECEMBER 26

In the family of God, there is literally nothing to fear. Hold onto hope, and you'll shine with it. Let go of hope and you'll fizzle out.

"I am the Alpha and the Omega,"
says the Lord God,
"who is and who was and
who is to come, the Almighty."
REVELATION 1:8

Like an attentive dad, our Father is right there. All the time. Sending little reminders of His love.

For what great nation is there
that has a god so near to it as is
the Lord our God whenever we call on Him?

DEUTERONOMY 4:7

The very best vessels for His kingdom are those who say, "OK, God...let's go after it! Use me however You want."

Be strong and courageous,
do not be afraid or tremble at them,
for the LORD your God is the one who goes with you.
He will not fail you or forsake you.
DEUTERONOMY 31:6

DECEMBER 29

Passionate people *may stumble a bit and learn as they go. But going after God will never, ever disappoint.*

How blessed is the man who does not walk
in the counsel of the wicked, nor stand in the path of sinners,
nor sit in the seat of scoffers!
But his delight is in the law of the Lord,
and in His law he meditates day and night.

PSALM 1:1-2

Like a butterfly whose D.N.A. still looks like the caterpillar's, the creature itself has been totally reborn. You are a new creation.

Therefore if anyone is in Christ,
he is a new creature; the old things passed away;
behold, new things have come.

II CORINTHIANS 5:17

Some people ask God for a single word or phrase as a theme for the upcoming year. If you ask for one and receive it, pay attention. He will lean in as you walk it out in faithfulness.

Thus says the Lord,
"Stand by the ways and see and ask for the ancient paths,
where the good way is, and walk in it;
and you will find rest for your souls."
JEREMIAH 6:16

Mfd. for © DaySpring
Siloam Springs, AR 72761
dayspring.com
Made in China

———

All rights reserved.
No part of this publication
may be reproduced, stored in a retrieval
system or transmitted in any form by
any means—electronic, mechanical,
photocopying, recording, or any other—
without the prior written permission
of the publisher.

—

Scripture taken from the
NEW AMERICAN STANDARD BIBLE®,
© Copyright The Lockman Foundation.
(www.lockman.org)

One Minute with God
Devotional Journal

ISBN-13: 978-1684085644
ISBN-10: 1684085640

9 781684 085644

10977

0 81983 66087 0